P9-BZS-123

DATE DUE			

FOOTBALL

AND ITS GREATEST PLAYERS

FOOTBALL

AND ITS GREATEST PLAYERS

EDITED BY MICHAEL ANDERSON

Britannica®
Educational Publishing
IN ASSOCIATION WITH

ROSEN
EDUCATIONAL SERVICES

Published in 2012 by Britannica Educational Publishing
(a trademark of Encyclopædia Britannica, Inc.)
in association with Rosen Educational Services, LLC
29 East 21st Street, New York, NY 10010.

Distributed exclusively by Rosen Educational Services.
For a listing of additional Britannica Educational Publishing titles, call toll free (800) 237-9932.

First Edition

Britannica Educational Publishing
Michael I. Levy: Executive Editor, Encyclopædia Britannica
J.E. Luebering: Director, Core Reference Group, Encyclopædia Britannica
Adam Augustyn: Assistant Manager, Encyclopædia Britannica

Anthony L. Green: Editor, Compton's by Britannica
Michael Anderson: Senior Editor, Compton's by Britannica
Sherman Hollar: Associate Editor, Compton's by Britannica

Marilyn L. Barton: Senior Coordinator, Production Control
Steven Bosco: Director, Editorial Technologies
Lisa S. Braucher: Senior Producer and Data Editor
Yvette Charboneau: Senior Copy Editor
Kathy Nakamura: Manager, Media Acquisition

Rosen Educational Services
Jeanne Nagle: Senior Editor
Nelson Sá: Art Director
Cindy Reiman: Photography Manager
Karen Huang: Photo Research
Matthew Cauli: Designer, Cover Design
Introduction by Jeanne Nagle

Library of Congress Cataloging-in-Publication Data

Football and its greatest players / edited by Michael Anderson.
   p. cm. — (Inside sports)
"In association with Britannica Educational Publishing, Rosen Educational Services."
Includes bibliographical references and index.
ISBN 978-1-61530-511-7 (library binding)
1. Football—United States—History—Juvenile literature. 2. Football players—United
States—Biography—Juvenile literature. I. Anderson, Michael, 1972-
GV950.7.F66 2012
796.332092—dc22

2011000082

Manufactured in the United States of America

On the cover, page 3: Drew Brees, quarterback of the NFL's New Orleans Saints, in 2010. *Chris Graythen/Getty Images*

Pages 6- 7, 85, 88, 91, 92 © www.istockphoto.com/brocreative;; pp. 10, 21, 37, 52, 61, 83 © www.istock-
photo.com/Mark Stahl; pp. 19, 32, 45, 46, 54© www.istockphoto.com/Mark Herreid; p. 53 (graphic)
© www.istockphoto.com/ Brandon Laufenberg; back cover, remaining interior background image
Shutterstock.com

CONTENTS

INTRODUCTION

I f Americans were to think of their brand of football as a product, it might be hard to decide if the sport is an import or an export. As evidence of the former, consider how modern gridiron football came to be. The game's roots reach back to 19th-century England, where rugby originated and became a popular pastime. Rugby, which can be described as a full-contact version of soccer that hinges on players carrying, rather than kicking, a ball, was imported to the United States in the late 1800s. Many East Coast colleges, including Yale and Princeton, formed teams that played a rugby-style game.

The game underwent a few changes once it came to the United States. Two of the most important early rule changes, dating from the 1880s, made the game more orderly. The first established a scrimmage, which awarded possession of the ball to one of the two teams, and the second created the system of downs, which required a team to advance the ball or lose possession of it. By 1920, gridiron football moved beyond the thriving college ranks and became a professional sport with the start of the National Football League (NFL). Gradually many of the rules and procedures of American football were adopted by Canadian teams, which up until then had mostly played a rugby-style game. American football also was "exported" to other countries beginning in 1991, first with the formation of a European professional league and later with the scheduling of NFL games abroad.

Whether it is an import or export, gridiron football today is a distinctly American sport. Virtually everything about the modern game was developed in the United States. The popularity of this type of football is undeniable. In some parts of the U.S., football fan devotion, particularly at the high school and college level, is so strong and sincere that the sport has been likened to a religion. College and professional games are televised every weekend and a few nights a week during the fall season. These broadcasts get good

A football on the field, awaiting kickoff. Shutterstock.com

ratings. Also, the Super Bowl, which is the NFL's championship game, is watched by an international television audience numbering in the tens of millions.

A big part of what makes gridiron football so popular is the personalities involved. Many players and coaches have contributed to making the game what it is today.

8

Modern-day Hall of Famers and current marquee players, including Emmitt Smith and Peyton Manning, respectively, are recognized by football fans around the globe.

Some names from the early days of football may not be as recognizable, but their contributions are certainly well known. For instance, Walter Camp, the coach who is considered the "Father of American Football," was the head of the rules committee that was formed soon after the game came to the United States. In addition to introducing the scrimmage and the system of downs, Camp was responsible for determining the dimensions of the playing field and the number of players on the field, among other fundamentals of the game.

Another coach, Glenn (Pop) Warner, has been honored for his accomplishments and innovations during his long career by having a national youth football program named after him. Pop Warner Youth Football, which operates programs in 42 states, emphasizes the development of game skills and academic excellence. In recognizing Coach Warner while also cultivating the next generation of players both on and off the field, the program connects football's past with its present and future.

The word football can mean many things, depending on where you are in the world. In North America it means gridiron football. The gridiron game, which takes its name from the distinctive line markings on the playing field, is a full contact game played primarily in the United States and Canada. It is known for violent collisions, high emotions, and spectacular athleticism. Gridiron football pits two teams against each other, each trying to move a ball into the other team's goal.

The game evolved from rugby in the late 1800s, and similarities between the two sports remain. There are obvious differences in equipment and rules, but the most important difference—the one that really began to separate the two sports—is the forward pass, which has been a part of football since 1906

but remains illegal in rugby. The American version of football is played on other continents, but the game has not established itself as a global sport.

FOOTBALL IN THE UNITED STATES

While baseball is traditionally regarded as America's national pastime, football has

Fans of the New Orleans Saints gather to cheer on their team during the 2007 NFC championship game. Football is an immensely popular sport in the United States. **Chris Graythen/Getty Images**

been for some time the country's most popular sport. It draws larger television audiences than does any other sport, and in parts of the country college games attract crowds that exceed 100,000. The championship game of professional football is the Super Bowl, which is the biggest annual American sports event.

Football is a highly organized sport in the United States. It is played at youth, high school, college, and professional levels. Various forms of recreational football also are very popular.

High Schools and Colleges

Football inspires passion at every level, but nowhere is this more true than at high schools and colleges. At these levels, local teams are often an important part of the community.

The schools in the National Collegiate Athletic Association (NCAA) are grouped into Divisions I, II, and III. Division I, which includes the major football powers, is further divided into two levels—I-A and I-AA. Most schools that meet Division I-A criteria belong to a conference made up of eight to 12 teams. Major I-A schools that are not in a conference are called independents.

In high school football, each state also has different conferences and divisions. All of the states hold championship tournaments in each division, and some states may have as many as eight divisions.

PROFESSIONAL LEAGUES

There is only one major professional league in the United States—the National Football League. However, the appetite for football in the United States is so great that rival professional leagues have been attempted, with mixed success. The professional Arena Football League plays an indoor version of football.

RECREATIONAL FOOTBALL

Recreational football has led to spin-off versions of the game that are less violent and can be played without pads and helmets. In touch football, the player with the ball is "tackled" simply by being touched by an opponent. Some teams play one-hand touch football and others play a two-handed version.

In flag football, all the players wear belts with plastic or cloth flags attached. The ballcarrier is considered stopped when an

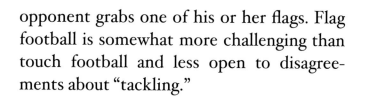

Rather than tackling each other, flag football players try to pull strips of material from the belt of the player who has the ball. **Shutterstock.com**

opponent grabs one of his or her flags. Flag football is somewhat more challenging than touch football and less open to disagreements about "tackling."

THE IMPACT OF TELEVISION

Few sports in the world have benefited from the arrival of television as much as professional football. In the 1950s leaders of college football worried that television coverage of games would drastically reduce attendance, and the NCAA held a tight rein on the number of games that could be broadcast. The NFL, under the leadership of commissioner Bert Bell, quickly embraced the new technology. The 1958 NFL Championship game between the Baltimore Colts and New York Giants was an overtime thriller that captivated a large national audience and is widely considered the turning point in the fortunes of the NFL.

Bell was succeeded as league commissioner in 1960 by Pete Rozelle, who would oversee one of the largest growth periods experienced by any sport. Rozelle increased the NFL's television revenues (television-generated income jumped from $350,000 per team in 1961 to $14 million per team in 1982) and established NFL Properties to manage the merchandising and marketing of the game. He also was responsible for the advent of Monday Night Football in 1970. The first regular primetime broadcast of a sporting event, Monday Night Football proved to be a major hit. As more games became available on television, interest in the sport grew.

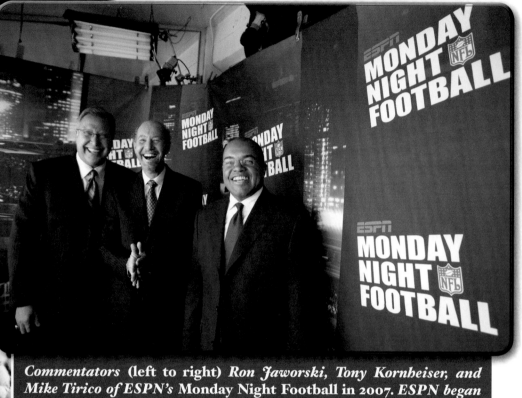

Commentators (left to right) *Ron Jaworski, Tony Kornheiser, and Mike Tirico of ESPN's* Monday Night Football *in 2007. ESPN began broadcasting the long-running program in 2006.* © AP Images

In the 1980s the NCAA changed its approach, making more college games available for broadcast on television. By the turn of the 21st century, college or pro football games aired daily from Thursday to Monday each week during the season. In 2003 the NFL launched its own 24-hour cable broadcast network.

FOOTBALL IN CANADA

Gridiron football in Canada is overshadowed by the national sport of ice hockey and has never attained the stature that the sport enjoys in the United States. Nonetheless, Canadian football enjoys a rich history. As in the United States, the game is played at youth, high school, college, and professional levels.

CANADIAN RUGBY UNION

Canadian football began with rugby games organized by athletic clubs and university students in Quebec and Ontario as early as the 1860s. The first football associations were formed a decade later, but it was the Canadian Rugby Union (CRU), formed in 1891, that rose to prominence. The CRU became the umbrella organization for provincial and regional unions that followed. Concerns about the rising influence of professionalism in club play lead collegiate teams to form a separate organization in 1897.

Canadian football officials were not as quick to pursue the commercial prospects of

A flag ceremony during a Canadian Football League (CFL) game. The CFL, which fielded eight teams in 2010, was formed by the merger of two rugby unions. Shutterstock.com

the sport as their counterparts in the United States, and for decades the sport drew few spectators. Clearly there was a desire to protect the amateurism of the sport as well as to preserve the game as one markedly different from American football. However, the influence of the American game was hard to deflect, and the rugby-style Canadian game gradually became more and more "Americanized."

RUGBY

According to legend, the sport of rugby began one afternoon in 1823 at England's Rugby School, when William Webb Ellis, playing soccer with his fellow students, picked up the ball and ran toward the goal. Though there is little historical fact to verify this story, it is true that the first rules of the game were written at the Rugby School in 1843.

The sport now thrives across the globe and is played by two different sets of rules—Rugby Union and Rugby League. Rugby is particularly popular in the British Isles, Australia, New Zealand, South Africa, and France.

An international rugby match between Wales and South Africa. Gallo Images/Getty Images

COLLEGE AND PROFESSIONAL LEVELS

Football at the college level continues in Canada but not with the sort of money and media attention lavished on college football in the United States. The game is currently governed by Canadian Interuniversity Sport, formed in 2001. Since 1967, top teams have met in the annual Canadian College Bowl, with the winner receiving the Vanier Cup.

On the professional level, the Canadian Football League (CFL) began in 1956 as the Canadian Football Council. It adopted its current name in 1958. As of 2010, the CFL had eight teams, four in the East Division and four in the West. Division champions compete for the Grey Cup, which was named for Governor-General Earl Grey and first awarded in 1909. The CFL took over stewardship of the cup from the CRU in 1966. The Grey Cup championship has since become one of Canada's most important sporting events.

Gridiron football in the United States is played by 11-man teams on a field 100 yards (91.4 meters) long and 160 feet (48.8 meters) wide with lines at 5-yard (4.6-meter) intervals along the 100-yard axis. An end zone extends 10 yards (9.14 meters) behind each goal line.

Parallel to the sidelines are two broken lines that designate where the ball is placed after it has been carried out of bounds. In college football these hash marks are 60 feet (18.29 meters) from each sideline; in professional games the distance from the sidelines is 70 feet 9 inches (21.56 meters).

The goalposts in high school and college football have different dimensions from those in the professional game. At all three levels, the goalposts are placed 10 yards (9.14 meters) behind the goal lines and the crossbar is 10 feet (3.05 meters) above the ground. In professional

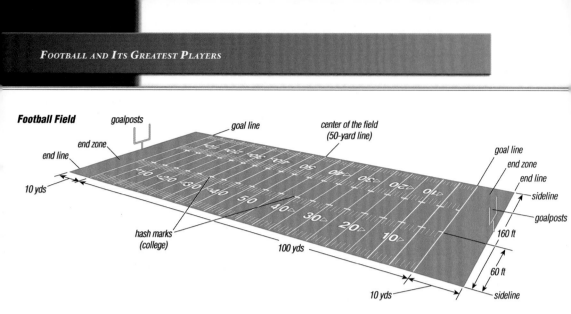

Football Field

goalposts
goal line
center of the field
(50-yard line)
end zone
end line
goal line
end zone
end line
10 yds
sideline
goalposts
hash marks
(college)
160 ft
100 yds
10 yds
60 ft
sideline

The dimensions, demarcation, and components of a football field. Encyclopædia Britannica, Inc.

football, however, the width between the posts is 18 feet 6 inches (5.64 meters), and the width in high school and college is 23 feet 4 inches (7.11 meters). The uprights of the goalposts in professional football extend 30 feet (9.14 meters) above the crossbar; in high school and college the uprights must be at least 20 feet (6.1 meters) in all.

EQUIPMENT

As football games got rougher, the equipment changed. Modern players wear plastic helmets and face masks, and pads to protect their shoulders, hips, thighs, knees,

Football helmet, shoulder pads, and cleats (spiked athletic shoes). As the game has gotten more physical and playing surfaces more advanced, the equipment has changed accordingly. Shutterstock.com

and forearms. Special pads and a flak jacket to cushion the ribs are worn for protection against specific injuries, and many players use a mouthpiece. The increased use of fields with artificial surfaces has resulted in a need for different kinds of cleated shoes to provide traction.

The playing uniform consists of a jersey and tight-fitting pants that end just below the knee. The use of numbers, now sewn on the front and back of the jerseys for identification, did not come into general practice until the 1920s.

RULES

The team that wins a coin toss before the game starts has its choice of kicking off or receiving the ball, or choosing the goal it will attack. The other team makes the choice to begin the second half.

THE KICKOFF

At the kickoff, the ball is placed on a rest called a tee and kicked to the opposing team. Kickoffs occur on the kicking team's 40-yard line in high school games, the 35-yard line in college play, and the 30-yard line in professional games. The receiving team must be at least 10 yards from the kickoff line, and any player on that team can advance the ball.

The ball is steadied on a tee in preparation for the kickoff. **Gene Lower/Getty Images**

If the ball is kicked all the way into the end zone, the receiving team, instead of running it out, can start play on the 20-yard line (a touchback). The kicking team can recover the ball once it has gone at least 10 yards and, in college and high school, as long as the ball has touched a member of the receiving team before it reaches the end zone. In addition to beginning the game, kickoffs take place after most scoring plays.

ADVANCING THE BALL

After the kickoff, the team with the ball tries to advance down the field for a score. The offensive team has four downs, or plays, in which to advance the ball at least 10 yards and thus make another first down. For each first down made, a team gets another series of four downs in which to gain at least 10 more yards.

Before each play begins, teams face each other on the line of scrimmage—an imaginary line that runs the width of the field and through the point to which the offensive team has advanced. After the ball is positioned, the center snaps, or passes, it through his legs, usually to the quarterback, who begins the play. The quarterback may run with the ball or decide to hand or pass it to a teammate, who, in turn, runs with it or passes it. Advancing the ball by running is also called rushing. The play ends when the ballcarrier is tackled, is forced out of bounds, or scores. If the play is an incomplete forward pass, the ball is returned to the line of scrimmage.

When a play begins, the offensive team must have at least seven players on the line of scrimmage. Players not on the line must be

The NFL's Cincinnati Bengals and Indianapolis Colts prepare for battle at the line of scrimmage during a game in 2010. Shutterstock.com

at least one yard behind it. At the snap of the ball, one player from the offensive backfield may be in motion, but only backward from or parallel to the line of scrimmage.

In most instances a team that has failed to gain 10 yards in three downs will, on fourth down, choose to punt the ball to the other team or attempt a field goal (described in the next section on Scoring). During a punt, the punter drops the ball and kicks it before it touches the ground. The opposing player who receives the ball cannot be interfered with before he touches it. The punt returner may run back with the ball or may signal for a fair catch, which prevents the opposing team from tackling him but also prevents the punt returner from advancing the ball after the catch is made.

Scoring

A player who carries the ball into the end zone or catches a forward pass there scores six points for a touchdown. The defensive team can get into scoring position with a turnover—by intercepting a pass, or by picking up a fumbled (dropped) ball. The team that scores a touchdown can attempt

a conversion, meaning extra points. One extra point is gained for kicking the ball over the crossbar of the goalposts. There is also the option of trying for a conversion by running or passing the ball into the end zone after a touchdown. This tactic scores two points. If a team is stopped short of the goal line, it can score a three-point field goal by kicking the ball over the crossbar of the goalposts. The defensive team may score a safety (worth two points) when the ballcarrier is downed in his own end zone or loses the ball out of bounds in his end zone, or if his team is penalized for committing a foul in its end zone.

After every scoring play except a safety, the scoring team kicks off to the other team. Following a safety, the team that has been scored on either kicks or punts from the 20-yard line.

OFFICIALS AND THE CLOCK

Games are managed by a team of seven officials—the referee (the leader of the officiating crew), umpire, linesman, field judge, back judge, line judge, and side judge. In professional and college games officials

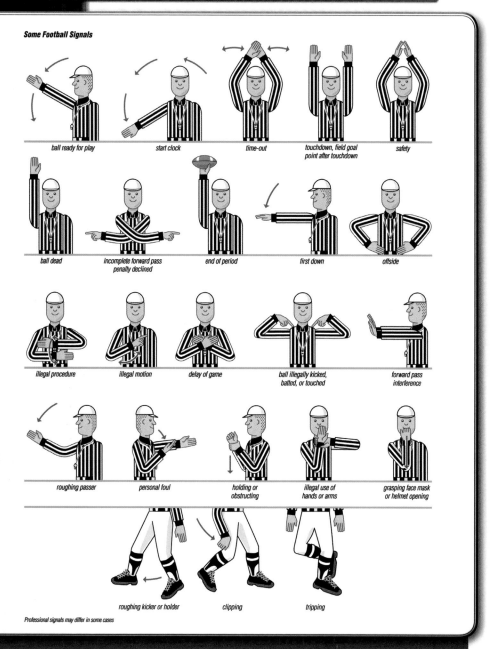

Some Football Signals

ball ready for play • start clock • time-out • touchdown, field goal point after touchdown • safety

ball dead • incomplete forward pass penalty declined • end of period • first down • offside

illegal procedure • illegal motion • delay of game • ball illegally kicked, batted, or touched • forward pass interference

roughing passer • personal foul • holding or obstructing • illegal use of hands or arms • grasping face mask or helmet opening

roughing kicker or holder • clipping • tripping

Professional signals may differ in some cases

Referees use hand signals to indicate what's happening on the field, particularly with regard to penalties. Encyclopædia Britannica, Inc.

may use instant replay technology to settle disputes regarding possession or spotting of the ball.

The officials penalize teams 5, 10, or 15 yards for most types of infractions. The most serious fouls, with 15-yard penalties, are clipping, or blocking from behind; spearing, or butting with the helmet; and roughing the passer, which is running into or tackling the passer after the ball has been thrown. Ten-yard penalties are usually for illegally holding an opposing player. Five-yard penalties are for minor infractions, such as delay of game, encroachment (making contact with an offensive player before the ball is snapped), and offside (crossing the line of scrimmage before the ball is snapped). Other penalties include loss of down for fouls committed by the offensive team and automatic first down for fouls committed by the defense.

A game is divided into four 15-minute quarters measured by an official clock. The clock is stopped on incomplete passes, when a runner goes out of bounds, and after a score. In college games, the clock stops after a first down until the officials reset the chains that are used to measure the 10-yard distance.

How Canadian Rules Differ

Although Canadian football has become less like rugby and more like football played in the United States, there are some basic differences. In Canada 12-man teams play on a field that is 110 yards (100.58 meters) long and 65 yards (59.44 meters) wide, with end zones 20 yards (18.29 meters) deep. The 12th player is used in the backfield on offense and as a linebacker (a player who lines up behind front-line defensive players) or pass defender on defense. A team is only allowed three downs in which to advance the ball 10 yards. Players are allowed to be in motion and moving toward the scrimmage line when the ball is snapped. In addition, a punt or a kickoff that enters the end zone must be advanced beyond the goal line by the receiving team or one point (a single) is awarded to the kicking team.

STRATEGY

Play on the field has undergone continual innovation. Through the years coaches have broken away from established strategies to introduce innovative formations or plays. In some cases these innovations have come in response to rule changes. In 1977, for example, landmark rule changes in the professional game gave the advantage to passing offenses. Among other things, the new rules banned defensive contact with wide receivers more than five yards downfield. With these changes, offenses began using the pass more than ever before, and defenses had to respond with new strategies.

DEFENSE

After defenders were prohibited from bumping pass receivers downfield, teams needed fast defensive backs who could keep up with the speedy receivers as well as extra defensive backs to cover them. The normal defensive alignment had called for four defensive backs, but coaches put as many as five or six on the field in obvious passing situations. Many teams began using only three defensive linemen, along with four linebackers—a defense considered strong against running plays, with the linebackers also helping on pass coverage.

However, even teams that used three defensive linemen switched to a four-man line in most passing situations to put added pressure on the opposing quarterback. A common practice in defensive football is the blitz, which refers to the use of linebackers and/or defensive backs to rush the quarterback. Teams will use blitzes in hopes of tackling the quarterback for a loss (known as a "sack") or forcing an errant throw that will be either incomplete or, better yet, intercepted.

OFFENSE

The offensive formation, or placement of the players at the line of scrimmage, has also changed. Today it is rare for teams to use the basic T formation, which places three running backs behind the quarterback and generates a strong but unspectacular ground attack. Some coaches now use this formation only when their team has just a few yards to gain, especially near the opponent's goal line.

The I formation has two backs in a straight line behind the quarterback. This type of offense usually features a running back and a blocking back. The split back formation, with two backs behind the quarterback, is designed for an offense with two strong runners. Spread offenses typically use only one running back and include a second tight end for blocking or a third receiver. In the spread

Some Offensive and Defensive Formations

I Formation (offense)

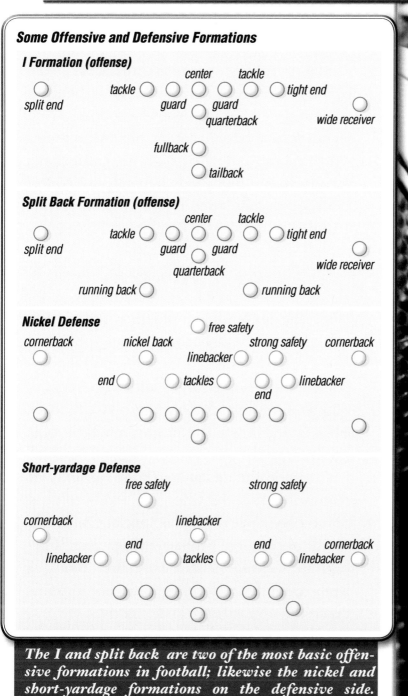

Split Back Formation (offense)

Nickel Defense

Short-yardage Defense

The I and split back are two of the most basic offensive formations in football; likewise the nickel and short-yardage formations on the defensive side. Encyclopædia Britannica, Inc.

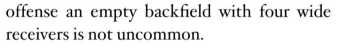

offense an empty backfield with four wide receivers is not uncommon.

On most plays, the quarterback takes the ball directly from the center for a handoff to a running back, or drops back and passes. In numerous passing situations many teams use the shotgun formation. The quarterback stands about five yards behind the center in order to gain time to watch as receivers attempt to break free from pass defenders.

USE OF SPECIALISTS

With the increasing sophistication of football, coaches began using various specialists in specific situations. On offense, such players include a second tight end, who may not be a good receiver but is an effective blocker, and a "third-down" running back, who is most productive as a receiver. On defense, specialists include the designated pass rusher, who comes in when the offense is likely to pass. Some players perform on special teams and rarely appear on offense or defense. They play in kicking situations, either blocking when their team returns a kick or running down the opposition's kick returner.

CHAPTER 3
THE COLLEGE GAME

Gridiron football was first a collegiate game, shaped largely by the elite universities in the Northeast. For decades schoolboys and college students organized informal games that were tolerated by administrators. In the 1820s students at Princeton University were playing a game they called "ballown," in which they used their fists and, later, their feet to advance the ball. The freshman and sophomore classes at Harvard competed in a type of football game on the first Monday of each school year, called Bloody Monday because the game was so rough. Organized football began earlier in high schools than in colleges, with games on Boston Common starting about 1860. A 17-year-old student organized the Oneida Football Club of Boston, which played between 1862 and 1865.

Early Games

Colleges began to organize football games after the American Civil War ended in 1865. The so-called Princeton rules were established in 1867, with 25 players on each team. The first football was patented that year. Rutgers College also established football rules in 1867, and its location, a short distance from Princeton, led the two schools into what has been called the first intercollegiate football game. It was played on Nov. 6, 1869, at Rutgers, but the game was actually more like soccer. Rutgers won that historic game, 6 goals to 4. For the next few years some colleges continued to play the soccer-type game.

In 1871 Harvard students began playing the so-called "Boston Game," which included elements of rugby (the player could pick up the ball and, if pursued, run with it) and soccer (kicking a round ball was still essential). Two years later representatives of Columbia, Princeton, Rutgers, and Yale met in New York City to formulate the first intercollegiate football rules for the soccer-style game. (Harvard chose not to attend because its playing rules were different.)

Next McGill University of Montreal challenged Harvard to a series of games. The

schools played two games at Harvard in the spring of 1874—the first with Harvard rules and the second with Canadian rugby rules, using the egg-shaped ball. After the McGill games, Harvard challenged Yale to a football game that was played under mixed soccer and rugby rules in November 1875. In 1876 Yale, Princeton, Harvard, and Columbia established the Intercollegiate Football Association, which set the size of the field at 140 by 70 yards (128 by 64 meters) and the number of players on a team at 15.

RULE CHANGES

The evolution from the rugby-style game to what became the modern game of American football began under the direction of Walter Camp, the Yale coach who is known as the Father of American Football. Yale had not officially joined the association until 1879 because it was holding out for 11-man teams. Led by Camp, the rules committee soon cut the number of players per side from 15 to 11. The committee also reduced the size of the field to 110 by 53 yards. In addition, Camp instituted a type of scrimmage in which a player snapped the ball back by kicking it to the quarterback. In 1882 Camp also

Walter Camp (left), *the Yale University coach who was instrumental in shaping the modern game of gridiron football.* Keystone-France/ Gamma-Keystone via Getty Images

introduced the system of downs. At first, a team had three plays, or downs, to advance the ball five yards or give up possession. The number of yards was changed to 10 in 1906, and the fourth down was added in 1912.

Tackling below the waist was legalized in 1888. Within a decade, concern about the increasing brutality of the game led some colleges to ban football. Mass plays, an offensive strategy that massed players on a single point of the defense—most famously in Harvard's "flying wedge" formation—had seriously injured nearly 180 players, including 18 who were killed. In 1905 U.S. President Theodore Roosevelt called on Harvard, Princeton, and Yale to help save the sport. Representatives of 13 eastern schools met at year-end and agreed on reforms. At a second meeting, attended by more than 60 schools, the group appointed a seven-member Football Rules Committee and set up the Intercollegiate Athletic Association, which five years later became the NCAA.

The new rule makers revolutionized football by legalizing the forward pass, which resulted in a more open style of play. They also prohibited mass plays, and teammates were prohibited from locking arms to clear a path for their ballcarrier. To further minimize mayhem, they shortened the length of the game from 70 to 60 minutes and established the neutral zone, which separates the teams by the length of the ball before each play begins.

COACHES WHO SHAPED THE COLLEGE GAME

The evolution of college football, in the style of play and the scope of fan worship, was realized mainly through the talents of several generations of innovative coaches. After Camp, one of the earliest trendsetters was Amos Alonzo Stagg, who coached at the University of Chicago from 1892 to 1932. Stagg originated many techniques, including the shifts of linemen and backs from one side to the other. His ends-back formation was considered the first of the mass plays.

Glenn S. (Pop) Warner had a 44-year coaching career that began at the University of Georgia in 1895. He introduced single- and double-wing systems of offense that dominated the sport for decades. The legendary Jim Thorpe played under Warner at Pennsylvania's Carlisle Indian Industrial School.

Perhaps the greatest motivator in collegiate history was Notre Dame's Knute Rockne, who was famed for his rousing halftime speeches. He was a respected tactician known for his contributions to the passing game and his refinement of the shift to the box formation. His teams of 1919, 1920, 1924, 1929, and 1930 won every game they played. The famous backfield of the 1924 team (Harry Stuhl-dreher, Jim Crowley, Elmer Layden, and Don Miller) was nicknamed the Four Horsemen by sports columnist Grantland Rice.

University of Notre Dame head coach Knute Rockne was known for his clever strategy, stirring motivational speeches, and string of winning seasons. **Library of Congress Prints and Photographs Division**

Bob Zuppke was known for the strong running attack of the University of Illinois teams that he built around the outstanding halfback Red Grange, the first player to be treated as a national idol on the strength of his sensational performances.

THE POSTWAR YEARS

Although many colleges were forced to abandon their football programs during World War II, the game continued to grow with the innovations of several top-notch coaches of the 1940s. Earl (Red) Blaik's Army teams of 1944, 1945, and 1946, which were undefeated, featured halfback Glenn Davis and fullback Felix (Doc) Blanchard. Blanchard, best known as "Mr. Inside," won the Heisman trophy as the outstanding college football player of 1945, and Davis, "Mr. Outside," received the award in 1946. In 17 years at Oklahoma (1947–63) Charles (Bud) Wilkinson had four undefeated teams and six teams that lost only one game.

Through the second half of the 20th century the college game continued to be dominated by legendary coaches. The coach of Ohio State for 28 seasons (1951–78), Woody Hayes led his teams to 13 Big Ten

RED GRANGE

Red Grange made football history as a halfback at the University of Illinois from 1923 to 1925. For his remarkable abilities to run and score, sportswriter Grantland Rice named him the Galloping Ghost.

Harold Edward Grange was born in Forksville, Pa., on June 13, 1903. He grew up there and in Wheaton, Ill. In his first season at Illinois he made 12 touchdowns and was named to Walter Camp's all-American team, an honor he was awarded again in the next two years.

In the 1924 season Grange was at his prime. Against the Big Ten champion University of Michigan team on October 18, he opened the game with a 100-yard kickoff return and scored three more times in the next 10 minutes. Illinois won the game by the score of 39–14. It was based on that day's feats that Rice gave Grange his nickname.

The 1925 season was somewhat of a disappointment, as the Illinois team was rather weak. After the season he left school and joined the Chicago Bears. With him on the team, the Bears drew huge crowds. His presence was a great asset to the National Football League, which was only four years old at the time.

In 1926 Grange played for football's New York Yankees, a team that disbanded in 1929. He was injured in 1927 and was forced to sit out the next season entirely. He rejoined the Bears in 1929 and continued playing until 1935. By then accumulated injuries and age were taking their toll.

Grange's income from professional football, as well as vaudeville and movie appearances, afforded him a comfortable retirement. He also became the first well-known athlete to become a successful radio and television broadcaster, with a career that spanned 25 years. In 1963 Grange was elected to the Football Hall of Fame. He died in Lake Wales, Fla., on Jan. 28, 1991.

championships and eight Rose Bowls (with four wins), and he developed 58 All-American players. After 21 years as Michigan's coach, Bo Schembechler resigned in 1989. Like Hayes, he won 13 Big Ten championships. Other champion coaches of the 1960s and 1970s were Ara Parseghian of Notre Dame, John McKay of Southern California, and Darrell Royal of Texas. Between 1958 and 1982, Paul (Bear) Bryant led Alabama to 232 wins and six national championships.

By the turn of the 21st century, the growing influence of television and professional football had begun to erode the dominance of coaches over the college game. Bobby Bowden of Florida State and Joe Paterno of Penn State—the two winningest

football coaches in NCAA Division I history—appeared to be the last of the major college coaches who would enjoy long, highly successful tenures at a single school.

Two major issues, cheating and racial segregation, occupied college football in the decades following World War II. In 1951 an academic cheating scandal at the U.S. Military Academy led to the expulsion of more than 80 cadets, many of them football players, and raised concerns about protecting the integrity of amateur athletics. Subsequently the NCAA gained greater powers to regulate and investigate athletic programs. In 1957 an agreement was reached to allow full scholarships for football players in order to reduce the influence of alumni and team boosters who had been making off-the-record payments to players.

African American players have been a part of the college game since the sport's beginnings. Early stars included Fritz Pollard of Brown University, Paul Robeson at Rutgers University, and Duke Slater at the University of Iowa. The segregation policies in the South applied to college football as well, and northern schools would typically sit their black players when they faced schools from the South. Black colleges began

Army head coach Earl Blaik (front, center) *with the team in March 1951. Later that year a cheating scandal rocked the U.S. Military Academy and cost the Army squad most of its players.* George Silk/ Time & Life Pictures/Getty Images

playing football in the 1890s, and new conferences and rivalries emerged a generation later. After professional baseball's race barrier was broken by Jackie Robinson in 1947 and professional football and basketball had begun integrating, pressure mounted on college sports to do the same. By the 1950s universities outside of the South began integrating and dropping games against segregated schools from their schedules. It was not until the 1960s that major universities in the South began integrating their teams.

BOWL GAMES

The Division I-A college football season is concluded with a series of bowl games. The first bowl game was the Rose Bowl, played in 1902 in Pasadena, Calif., between Michigan and Stanford. It became an annual game in 1916. In the 1930s other major bowls were founded, including the Orange Bowl in Miami and the Sugar Bowl in New Orleans. By the early 21st century, there were more than 30 bowl games. Bowls are played beginning in mid-December, with the most prominent bowl games held in early January.

Bowl games have always been an important part of determining a national champion

Rose Bowl stadium, located in Pasadena, Calif. The Rose Bowl has been played every year since 1902. Shutterstock.com

of college football. In the past, the results of the bowls were considered by selected coaches and sportswriters who would vote in separate polls to determine the national champion. As one might expect, the sportswriters' poll and the coaches' poll often named two different champions. The lower divisions of college football conclude their season with a play-off to determine a national champion, and many fans have called for a

play-off system for Division I-A. However, the tradition and financial benefits of bowl games have made the major colleges reluctant to adopt a play-off system.

In 1998 the Bowl Championship Series (BCS) was introduced as a solution to the problem of determining a true national champion. The BCS uses a complex equation that factors in each team's win-loss record, the strength of its schedule, its ranking in the two polls, and its standing in several computer rankings, and assigns a score to each team. The top two teams in the BCS standings at the end of the regular season are placed in the national championship game. At first the championship game rotated each year between the four major bowls (Rose, Orange, Sugar, and Fiesta). In 2006, however, the BCS National Championship Game was established as a fifth, stand-alone game within the BCS.

CHAPTER 4

THE PROFESSIONAL GAME

Though there have been professional football teams since the 1890s, the premier professional league, the National Football League (NFL), began in 1920 as the American Professional Football Association. After one year the league was re-organized, and in 1922 it took its current name.

THE NFL

The NFL consists of two conferences, the American and the National. The conferences originated with the merger of the NFL's 16 teams with 10 from a rival professional league, the American Football League (AFL), between 1966 and 1970. Out of the merger also came the Super Bowl, in which the conference champions play each other at the end of each season to determine the league champion.

TEAMS OF THE NFL

AFC East
Buffalo Bills
Miami Dolphins
New England Patriots
New York Jets

NFC East
Dallas Cowboys
New York Giants
Philadelphia Eagles
Washington Redskins

AFC North
Baltimore Ravens
Cincinnati Bengals
Cleveland Browns
Pittsburgh Steelers

NFC North
Chicago Bears
Detroit Lions
Green Bay Packers
Minnestona Vikings

AFC South
Houston Texans
Indianapolis Colts
Jacksonville Jaguars
Tennessee Titans

NFC South
Atlanta Falcons
Carolina Pathers
New Orleans Saints
Tampa Bay Buccaneers

AFC West
Denver Broncos
Kansas City Chiefs
Oakland Raiders
San Diego Chargers

NFC West
Arizona Cardinals
St. Louis Rams
San Francisco 49ers
Seattle Seahawks

"GENTLEMEN'S AGREEMENT"

The NFL was originally a racially integrated league, but a "gentlemen's agreement" orchestrated by Boston (now Washington) Redskins owner George Preston Marshall in 1934 banned African Americans from the league. The reintegration began soon after the end of World War II when Kenny Washington joined the Los Angeles Rams and Marion Motley joined the Cleveland Browns. Professional football was fully integrated by 1962.

The NFL subsequently went through two more rounds of expansion. By 2002 the NFL was a 32-team league. At that time the league was aligned into two conferences with four divisions in each and four teams in each division.

LAMBEAU AND HALAS

Two of the founding fathers of professional football were Earl (Curly) Lambeau of the Green Bay Packers and George Halas of the Chicago Bears. Lambeau's 29 consecutive years as a head coach with Green Bay (he left the team in 1949 after winning six NFL titles) remained a professional record into

Legendary Chicago Bears coach and owner George Halas. Robert Riger/Getty Images

the 1990s. The founder, owner, and first head coach of the Bears, Halas was responsible for reviving the T formation, which replaced the single wing as the game's dominant offensive system. Halas also helped introduce such innovations to the game as public announcement systems and radio broadcasts.

OTHER INFLUENTIAL COACHES

Other coaches who introduced important changes to the professional game include Paul Brown, who coached the Cleveland Browns to three NFL titles and was the first coach to scout opposing teams. Sid Gillman of the Los Angeles Rams was credited with developing the high-powered passing offenses that helped popularize pro football.

Vince Lombardi, known for his motivational success and discipline, reaffirmed the stature of the Green Bay Packers with five NFL championships and victories in the first

Dallas Cowboys coach Tom Landry, wearing his trademark fedora on the sidelines during a game against the San Diego Chargers in 1986. Ken Levine/Getty Images

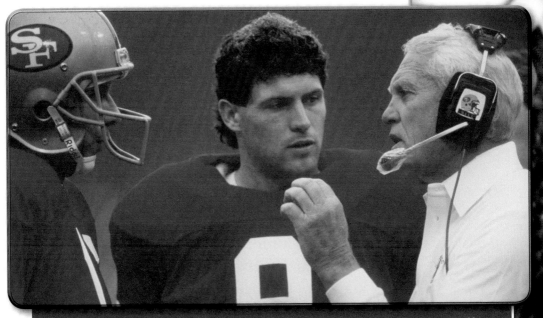

Bill Walsh (right), *head coach of the San Francisco 49ers, talks to quarterback Joe Montana* (left) *and the team's backup quarterback, Steve Young* (center), *in 1987.* Otto Greule Jr./Getty Images

two Super Bowls (1966, 1967). Chuck Noll coached the Pittsburgh Steelers to four Super Bowl titles in the 1970s. Don Shula, the winningest coach in NFL history with more than 300 victories, led the Miami Dolphins to an undefeated season in 1972 and six Super Bowls, winning two.

Highly successful and innovative coaches of the 1970s and '80s include Tom Landry, who won two Super Bowls as head coach of the Dallas Cowboys and invented the 4-3 defense, and Bill Walsh, who guided the

San Francisco 49ers to three Super Bowl victories and is credited with developing the ball-control passing game known as the West Coast offense.

OTHER PROFESSIONAL LEAGUES

The NFL has periodically faced challenges from other professional football leagues. These rivals have included the All-America Football Conference (AAFC, 1946–49), the American Football League (AFL, 1960–69), and the World Football League (1974–75). Two AAFC teams joined the NFL in 1950, and a merger of the AFL with the NFL was completed in 1970. The United States Football League was launched in 1983, but was forced to end play after two seasons. The Arena Football League, an indoor league with eight-man teams, debuted in 1987.

Despite the failures of earlier rivals, the NFL backed a new international league in

The Frankfurt Galaxy and the Hamburg Sea Devils play in what turned out to be the last championship game for NFL Europe, in 2007. The league disbanded shortly afterward. **Lars Baron/Bongarts/Getty Images**

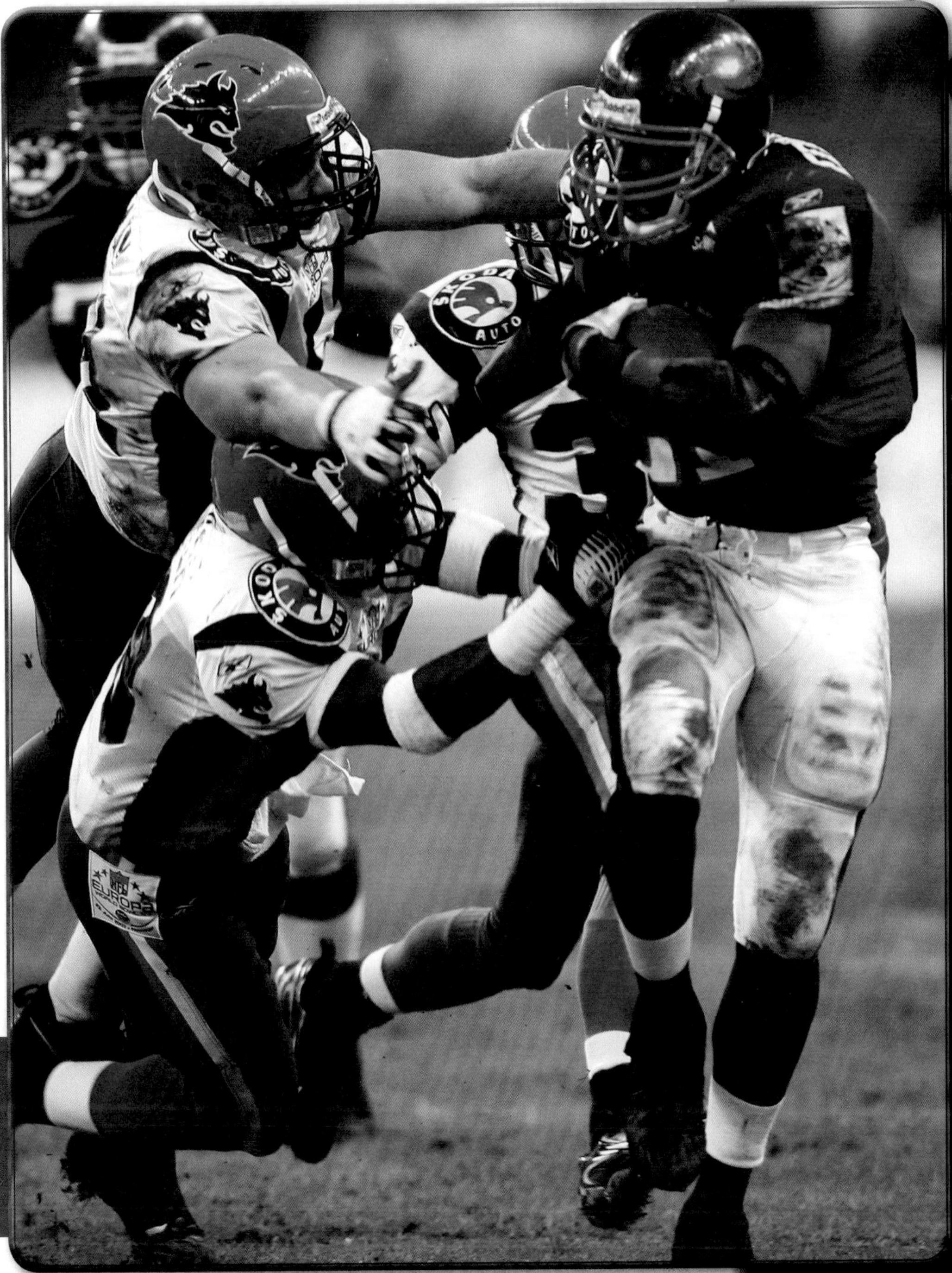
SKODA
AUTO

1991. For two seasons the World League of American Football (WLAF) had teams in the United States, Europe, and Canada. The WLAF was inactive in 1993–94, but it returned in 1995 with only European teams. Before the 1998 season, the league's name was changed to NFL Europe. The NFL discontinued the league in 2007 and decided instead to focus on staging regular-season NFL games in other countries.

CHAPTER 5
NOTABLE PLAYERS

Football players, like those of other sports, are most readily measured by their statistics—their rushing or passing yards, for example, or their number of touchdown receptions. However, players also can be measured by the performance of their teams. The players profiled here, both Hall of Famers and contemporary stars, hold a great number of records for their individual achievements. What makes many of them even more notable is the way they have helped elevate their teams to the NFL's elite.

HALL OF FAMERS

Players, coaches, and owners who have made outstanding contributions to the game of gridiron football earn entry into the Football Hall of Fame, located in Canton, Ohio. A few standout individuals from several decades are profiled in this section.

BART STARR

Quarterback Bart Starr was a great leader and field tactician. He led the Green Bay Packers to five league championships (1961–62, 1965–67) and to Super Bowl victories after the 1966 and 1967 seasons.

Bryan Bartlett Starr was born on Jan. 9, 1934, in Montgomery, Ala. From 1952 to 1955 he was quarterback for the University of Alabama, completing eight of 12 passes in the 1953 Orange Bowl victory over Syracuse and directing the team to a loss in the 1954 Cotton Bowl. He was drafted in the 17th round by the Packers in 1956 and played with them through the 1971 season. He became the team's starting quarterback in 1959, the first season Vince Lombardi coached the Packers.

Starr was particularly effective in post-season games. In six NFL title games, he completed 84 of 145 passes attempted for 1,090 yards, with only one interception. His performance in his two Super Bowl games was outstanding, and he was named most valuable player in both of them. Four times All-NFL (1961–62, 1964, 1966), he led the league in percentage of passes completed four times (1962, 1966, and 1968–69) and average yards gained three times (1966–68).

Green Bay Packers quarterback Bart Starr. Focus On Sport/ Getty Images

After retiring as a player in 1972, Starr became head coach of the Packers from 1975 through 1983. However, his coaching success did not equal his success as a player. He was elected to the Pro Football Hall of Fame in 1977.

JIM BROWN

The dominant player of his era, Jim Brown led the NFL in rushing yards for eight of his nine seasons. He ranks among the best running backs of all time.

James Nathaniel Brown was born in St. Simons, Ga., on Feb. 17, 1936. In high school and at Syracuse University in New York, he displayed exceptional all-around athletic ability, excelling in basketball, baseball, track, and lacrosse as well as football. In his final year at Syracuse, Brown earned All-America honors in both football and lacrosse.

From 1957 through 1965 Brown played for the Cleveland Browns of the NFL. During that time he led the league in rushing yardage every year except 1962. He ran for more than 1,000 yards in seven seasons and established NFL single-season records by rushing for 1,527 yards in 1958 (12-game schedule) and 1,863 yards in 1963 (14-game schedule),

Running back Jim Brown of the Cleveland Browns, finding a gap in the defense and gaining yardage. Walter Iooss Jr./Sports Illustrated/ Getty Images

a record broken by O.J. Simpson of the Buffalo Bills in 1973. On Nov. 24, 1957, he set an NFL record by rushing for 237 yards in a single game, and he equaled that total on Nov. 19, 1961. At the close of his career, he had scored 126 touchdowns, gained a record 12,312 rushing yards, and a record combined yardage (rushing along with pass receptions) of 14,811 yards. Brown's rushing and combined yardage records stood until 1984, when both were surpassed by Walter Payton of the Chicago Bears.

At 30 years of age and seemingly at the height of his athletic abilities, Brown retired from football to pursue a career in motion pictures. He appeared in many action and adventure films, among them *The Dirty Dozen* (1967) and *100 Rifles* (1969). Brown also was active in issues facing African Americans, forming groups to assist black-owned businesses and to rehabilitate gang members. He was elected to the Pro Football Hall of Fame in 1971.

JERRY RICE

Many consider Jerry Rice to be the greatest wide receiver in the history of the NFL. Playing primarily for the San Francisco 49ers, he set a host of NFL records, including those for career touchdowns (208), receptions (1,549), and reception yardage (22,895).

Born Jerry Lee Rice on Oct. 13, 1962, in Starkville, Miss., he attended Mississippi Valley State University in Itta Bena on a football scholarship. There he earned All-America honors and set 18 records in Division I-AA of the National Collegiate

Jerry Rice of the San Francisco 49ers was equally good at short-pass plays and acrobatic catches of long throws, like this touchdown reception in 1991. **Brad Mangin/Sports Illustrated/Getty Images**

Athletic Association, including most catches in a single game (24).

Rice was drafted by the San Francisco 49ers in the first round of the 1985 NFL draft. He struggled at first, but in his second season he caught 86 passes and led the league in reception yardage (1,570) and touchdown receptions (15). Rice thrived in San Francisco's so-called West Coast offense, which relied on many short, quick passes by the quarterback and precise route running by the receivers. He set a single-season record for touchdown receptions (22) in 1987, even though a players' strike limited the season to 12 games, and was named NFL Player of the Year. Led by Rice and quarterback Joe Montana, the 49ers won the Super Bowl at the end of the 1988, 1989, and 1994 seasons. Rice was named the most valuable player of Super Bowl XXIII (1988 season), and he set numerous Super Bowl records. He was named to the annual Pro Bowl from 1986 through 1998.

In a controversial move to develop younger players, the 49ers traded Rice to the Oakland Raiders before the 2001 season. The following season he became the first player to score more than 200 career touchdowns as he helped the Raiders reach Super Bowl XXXVII, where they were defeated

by the Tampa Bay Buccaneers. In 2003 he made his 13th Pro Bowl appearance. Midway through the 2004 season, Rice was traded to the Seattle Seahawks, but he was released by the team at the end of the season. After an unsuccessful attempt to become a starting receiver for the Denver Broncos the following year, he signed a ceremonial one-day contract with San Francisco and retired as a 49er. Rice was inducted into the Pro Football Hall of Fame in 2010.

EMMITT SMITH

In 2002 Emmitt Smith became the all-time leading rusher in NFL history. He retired after the 2004 season with 18,355 yards rushing. He also holds the record for most rushing touchdowns in a career, with 164.

Emmitt James Smith III was born in Pensacola, Fla., on May 15, 1969. He played football for three years (1987–89) at the University of Florida (in Gainesville), racking up 58 school records before being selected in the first round of the NFL draft by the Dallas Cowboys. Smith soon established himself as one of the league's premier running backs. He was named NFL Offensive Rookie Of The Year in 1990. The following season he

Emmitt Smith at his Hall of Fame induction ceremony. **Joe Robbins/ Getty Images**

ran for 1,563 yards to capture the first of his four NFL rushing titles (the other three were in 1992, 1993, and 1995). He led the Cowboys to back-to-back Super Bowl wins following the 1992 and 1993 seasons. In 1993 he earned most valuable player trophies for both the regular season and the Super Bowl. A third Super Bowl championship followed the 1995 season. After the 2002 season Smith was released by the Cowboys and signed by the Arizona Cardinals.

Though Smith was relatively small—he stood only 5 feet 9 inches (1.75 meters) tall and weighed 212 pounds (96 kilograms)—and lacked great speed, he thrived in the NFL by relying on his strength, doggedness, and superb conditioning. He ultimately proved to be one of the NFL's most durable players at any position; between 1990 and 2002 he failed to start in only two games. In 2010 he was inducted into the Pro Football Hall of Fame.

CONTEMPORARY PLAYERS

Still active in the pro game as of the 2010 season, the individuals featured in this section are marquee players, performers who stand out over the rest because of their skill and popularity. These men may very well be elected to the Hall of Fame when their playing days are through.

BRETT FAVRE

Known for his agility, competitiveness, and field presence, Brett Favre broke all the major NFL career passing records as quarterback of the Green Bay Packers. He was also remarkably durable, setting the record for most consecutive starts by an NFL quarterback.

Brett Lorenzo Favre was born on Oct. 10, 1969, in Gulfport, Miss. He grew up in Kiln, Miss., and attended the University of Southern Mississippi, where he became the football team's starting quarterback while a freshman. He was drafted by the NFL's Atlanta Falcons in 1991 but was traded to Green Bay the following year. Originally a backup quarterback, he started for an injured teammate in the third game of the 1992 season and never gave up the position. Favre was named the league's most valuable player (MVP) a record three consecutive times (1995, 1996, 1997) and led the league in touchdown passes in each MVP year.

At the end of the 1996 season, Favre led the Packers to victory over the New England Patriots in Super Bowl XXXI. He returned to the Super Bowl a year later, but the Packers lost. The team was less successful in the following years, but Favre continued to be productive. He led the league in pass completions in 1998 and 2005, and he had the most passing yards and touchdown passes in 1998 and 2003, respectively. In the 2007 season Favre broke John Elway's record of 148 career wins as a starting quarterback and Dan Marino's all-time records of 420 touchdown passes and 61,371 passing yards.

Quarterback Brett Favre, in action with the Green Bay Packers.
Jonathan Daniel/Getty Images

Favre announced his retirement at the end of the 2007 NFL season.

In mid-2008 Favre let it be known that he wanted to return to the NFL, and he was reinstated by the league. The Packers traded him to the New York Jets. Though he was named to his 10th career Pro Bowl in 2008, Favre's one season with the Jets was nevertheless a disappointment. He led the league in interceptions, and the Jets missed the play-offs.

Favre retired for the second time in early 2009. Later that year, however, he again returned to the league and joined the Minnesota Vikings. Favre had one of his best seasons in 2009. He set a career high in completion percentage and threw only seven interceptions. He guided the Vikings to a 12–4 record and the National Conference championship game After the 2010 season Favre announced his retirement a third time.

Peyton Manning

Quarterback Peyton Manning was named the NFL most valuable player (MVP) four times in his first 12 NFL seasons. He led the Indianapolis Colts to a Super Bowl victory in 2007.

Born on March 24, 1976, in New Orleans, La., Peyton Williams Manning was immersed in football from a very young age. His father, Archie Manning, was a star quarterback with the New Orleans Saints. (Younger brother Eli also became an NFL quarterback.) Peyton Manning attended the University of Tennessee, where he was the starting quarterback for four years. He earned the Sullivan Award as the country's top amateur athlete in 1996, was selected a first-team All-American in 1997, and finished his collegiate career in 1998 as Tennessee's career passing leader.

Manning was drafted first overall by the Indianapolis Colts in 1998. After struggling somewhat in his rookie season, he helped the Colts in 1999 to win the franchise's first division title since 1987. In 2000 Manning threw for 4,413 yards and 33 touchdowns to finish among the NFL's leading passers. Three years later he shared the league's MVP award with Steve McNair of the Tennessee Titans. Manning won the MVP honor outright in 2004 with a sensational performance that included 49 touchdown passes, an NFL record for a single season. (His touchdown record was broken by Tom Brady in 2007.)

During the 2005 season, Manning led the Colts to victories in their first 13 games.

Indianapolis Colts quarterback Peyton Manning is one of the most talented and popular players in the NFL. **Andy Lyons/Getty Images**

Although considered one of the favorites to win the Super Bowl, the team lost in the divisional play-offs. Some questioned Manning's ability to win a championship, but in the 2006 season he silenced his critics. He threw for 4,397 yards — the seventh time in his career he had passed for more than 4,000 yards, breaking the record held by the Miami Dolphins' Dan Marino — and helped the Colts defeat the Chicago Bears in Super Bowl XLI. For his performance, which included 25 completed passes for 247 yards, Manning was named the game's MVP. In 2008 and 2009 he won his third and fourth league MVP awards.

After the 2009 season Manning led the Colts to the Super Bowl once again, but his team lost to the New Orleans Saints.

Randy Moss

Wide receiver Randy Moss was a key player on some of the most productive offensive teams in NFL history. He befuddled defenders with his incredible speed and outstanding leaping ability.

Randy Gene Moss was born on Feb. 13, 1977, in Rand, W. Va. He played college football at Marshall University in West Virginia, then a member of Division I-AA

Randy Moss in 2003, doing what he does best—catching a touchdown pass. **Brian Bahr/Getty Images**

of the NCAA. In his freshman season he set a number of I-AA receiving records and helped lead Marshall to a national championship. During his sophomore year Marshall moved up to Division I-A, and Moss set a I-A record by catching 25 touchdown passes. In the 1998 NFL draft Moss was selected in the first round by the Minnesota Vikings.

Moss was a sensation in his first year with the Vikings. He set an NFL rookie record with 17 receiving touchdowns, was named NFL Offensive Rookie Of The Year, and earned first-team All-Pro honors. Minnesota scored the most points in NFL history that season and posted a 15–1 record before losing in the National Conference championship game. Moss caught at least 11 touchdown passes and amassed at least 14,000 receiving yards in each of the following two seasons, and he set career highs with 111 receptions for 1,632 yards in the 2003–04 season.

In 2005 the Vikings traded Moss to the Oakland Raiders. His two years in Oakland were unproductive by his standards. Moss scored only 11 total touchdowns in his two seasons with the Raiders, and he was traded to the New England Patriots in 2007.

Moss turned his career around in New England. In 2007–08 he teamed with quarter-back Tom Brady to form the core of a high-powered offense that broke the single-season scoring mark, previously held by the Minnesota Vikings, while posting the first 16–0 regular-season record in NFL history. In addition, Moss broke Jerry Rice's 20-year-old NFL record by catching 23 touchdown passes. However, the Patriots' storybook run ended with an upset loss to the New York Giants in the Super Bowl.

In 2009 Moss caught his 141st career touchdown pass, the second highest total in NFL history behind Rice. During the 2010 season Moss played for both the Vikings and the Tennessee Titans.

LaDainian Tomlinson

At 5 feet 10 inches (1.8 meters) and about 220 pounds (100 kilograms), LaDainian Tomlinson was considered small for an NFL running back. But what he lacked in size, he made up for with a hard-nosed running style and terrific speed in the open field. After just his first few years in the league, the player many fans referred to as LT could already stake a claim as one of the premier running backs of his era.

Tomlinson was born on June 23, 1979, in Rosebud, Tex. He attended Texas Christian University in Fort Worth, and in both his junior and senior years he was college football's leading rusher. In 2000 he finished fourth in the voting for the Heisman Trophy, given to the year's outstanding collegiate player. He was selected by the San Diego Chargers in the first round of the NFL draft in 2001.

Tomlinson was one of the most versatile players in the NFL, gaining more than 1,200

Running back LaDainian Tomlinson was a double threat for seven seasons with the San Diego Chargers, breaking records in both rushing yards and pass receptions. **Donald Miralle/Getty Images**

rushing yards, and making more than 50 pass receptions in each of his first seven seasons. In 2003 he became the only NFL player ever to rush for 1,000 yards and catch 100 passes in the same season. Also in that season, he became one of only seven players in the history of the league to have run, caught, and passed for a touchdown in a single game.

In 2006 Tomlinson led the league in rushing yards and broke both Shaun Alexander's record for most touchdowns scored in one season (31) and the 46-year-old record for most single-season points scored (186). Earlier in the season Tomlinson had reached another milestone when he scored the 100th touchdown of his NFL career, accomplishing the feat in just 89 games—quicker than anyone else in league history. Tomlinson's success led to his selection as the NFL's most valuable player for the 2006 season.

Tomlinson led the NFL in rushing yards and rushing touchdowns again in the 2007 season, and in the postseason he helped the Chargers advance to the American Conference championship game. However, his numbers declined over the following two seasons; in 2009 he rushed for a career-low 730 yards. In 2010 he was released by San Diego and signed with the New York Jets.

CONCLUSION

For millions of Americans, autumn is synonymous with football. On campuses across the country, the game and its accompanying spectacle—bands and cheerleaders, mascots and pep rallies, bonfires and homecoming celebrations—are an integral part of the high school and college experience. For fans of pro football, Sunday has long been game day, as hundreds of thousands of spectators gather to cheer their teams in stadiums while millions more watch on television. Super Bowl Sunday, the pinnacle of the NFL season, has become an unofficial national holiday, as famous for the surrounding hoopla as for the game itself.

Despite this great enthusiasm in the United States, football has not been taken up in the rest of the world to the same degree as other American sports such as basketball and baseball. For most people outside the United States, "football" is still the sport that Americans call soccer. Beginning in the 1980s, however, gridiron football teams and leagues were established in Europe, and the game achieved a degree of international popularity through television. The NFL entered a new era in 2005 when the first regular-season NFL game outside the United States was played in Mexico City. Huge crowds attended this game as well as later games in London, indicating an unprecedented level of international interest in this very American sport.

backfield The football players whose positions are behind the line of scrimmage, or the positions themselves.

blitz In football, a rush of the passer by a defensive linebacker, back, or end.

center The football player on the offense in the middle of the line who passes the ball between his legs to a back to start a down.

conversion A successful attempt for a point or points after a touchdown; also used to describe attempts to gain a new set of downs and continue offensive play.

down A complete play to advance the ball in football.

field goal In football, a scoring play of three points, made by kicking the ball over the crossbar and between the goalposts.

fullback An offensive football back used primarily for line plunges and blocking.

gridiron Football field, so named for the parallel yard lines marking the rectangular field.

halfback One of the backs stationed near either flank in football.

infraction A violation of the rules, resulting in a penalty.

linebacker A defensive football player who lines up immediately behind the line of scrimmage to make tackles on running plays through the line or defend against short passes.

punt To kick with the top of the foot before the ball, which is dropped from the hands, hits the ground.

quarterback The player on offense who usually lines up behind the center, calls the signals, and directs the offensive play of the team. The quarterback is also the primary forward passer.

sack Tackling the quarterback behind the line of scrimmage

scrimmage The interplay between two football teams that begins with the snap of the ball and continues until the ball is dead.

segregation Forcefully keeping one class of group of individuals separate and treating them differently.

spotting In football, placing the ball at a specific spot where play has ended.

tackle To grab and stop the forward progress of a player on the offense who is in possession of the ball.

tactician Someone who makes plans and devises strategy.

tight end An offensive football end who lines up close to the tackle and can act as a lineman or receiver.

turnover The act or instance of the offense losing possession of the ball through interception, fumble, or a failure to convert a set of downs.

wide receiver A football receiver who normally lines up several yards to the side of the offensive formation.

Canadian Football League (CFL)
50 Wellington Street East, 3rd Floor
Toronto, ON M5E 1C8
Canada
(416) 322-9650
Web site: http://www.cfl.ca
The CFL is Canada's professional football
league. The site provides information
on game schedules, teams, and player
statistics.

Football Canada
100-2255 Boulevard St. Laurent
Ottawa, ON K1G 4K3
Canada
(613) 564-0003
Web site: http://www.footballcanada.com
Football Canada is the national governing
body of amateur football in Canada.
The site provides information on teams
and players throughout the coun-
try as well as the Long-Term Athlete
Development Model.

National Football Foundation and College
Hall of Fame
433 E. Las Colinas Boulevard, Suite 1130
Irving, TX, 75039
(972) 556-1000

Web site: http://www.footballfoundation.org

The mission of the National Football Foundation is to promote amateur football as a way to develop the qualities of leadership, sportsmanship, competitive zeal, and the drive for academic excellence.

National Football League (NFL)
280 Park Avenue
New York, NY 10017
(212) 450-2000
Web site: http://www.nfl.com

The NFL site provides information on game schedules, teams, and player statistics. Information on its youth tackle division and High School Player Development camps is also available.

Pro Football Hall of Fame
2121 George Halas Drive NW
Canton, OH 44708
(330) 456-8207
Web site: http://www.profootballhof.com

The Pro Football Hall of Fame's collection of artifacts, photographs, and more helps recount the history of football in the United States. Activity guides for students and information on the various

events and workshops the Hall of Fame hosts is also available.

USA Football
45 N. Pennsylvania Street, Suite 700
Indianapolis, IN 46204
(317) 614-7750
Web site: http://www.usafootball.com
USA Football provides information on a
    wealth of topics, from tips and drills to
    balancing academics and athletics. It also
    offers a Player Academy to help develop
    fundamentals among youth interested in
    playing football.

WEB SITES

Due to the changing nature of Internet links, Rosen Educational Services has developed an online list of Web sites related to the subject of this book. This site is updated regularly. Please use this link to access the list:

http://www.rosenlinks.com/spor/foot

Barber, Phil, and John Fawaz. *NFL's Greatest: Pro Football's Best Players, Teams, and Games*, 2nd ed. (DK, 2002).

Biskup, Agnieszka. *Football: How It Works* (Capstone, 2010).

Freeman, Mike. *Bloody Sundays: Inside the Dazzling, Rough-and-Tumble World of the NFL* (W. Morrow, 2003).

MacCambridge, Michael. *America's Game: The Epic Story of How Pro Football Captured a Nation* (Random House, 2004).

Madden, John, with Bill Gutman. *John Madden's Heroes of Football: The Story of America's Game* (Dutton Children's Books, 2006).

McCullough, Bob. *My Greatest Day in Football: The Legends of Football Recount Their Greatest Moments* (Thomas Dunne Books/St. Martin's Press, 2001).

The Official National Football League Record and Fact Book (Time, annual).

Watterson, John Sayle. *College Football: History, Spectacle, Controversy* (Johns Hopkins Univ. Press, 2000).

Whittingham, Richard. *Rites of Autumn: The Story of College Football* (Free Press, 2001).

Wingate, Brian. *Football: Rules, Tips, Strategy, and Safety* (Rosen, 2007).

INDEX

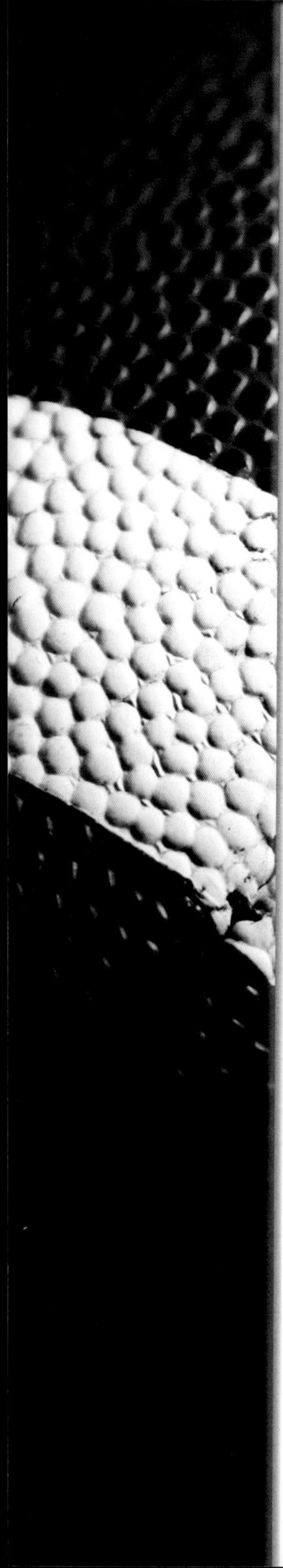

W

Z